D1505663

THE INFINITE
ROSE

HAROLD FEINSTEIN

BULFINCH PRESS

AOL TIME WARNER BOOK GROUP · BOSTON · NEW YORK · LONDON

For Lamont Thompson
in memory of Betty Thompson

ACKNOWLEDGMENTS

I wish to thank the following people: Mike Lowe for his extraordinary experience with and generous advice about roses; Lance Hidy for his exquisite design sense and perpetual input in the editing; Cindia Sanford, whose personal involvement with and love of all flowers has been a constant inspiration.

I also want to thank Jill Cohen, publisher, and Michael Sand, editor, at Bulfinch for their enthusiastic efforts on behalf of this book.

My wife and soulmate, Judith, for her warmth, wisdom, and love.

Lastly, I want to thank Fabia Barsic-Ochoa and Dan Steinhardt of Epson America, whose printers and scanners made this project feasible. HF

Copyright © 2004 by Harold Feinstein

All rights reserved. No part of this book may be reproduced in any form or by any electronic or mechanical means, including information storage and retrieval systems, without permission in writing from the publisher, except by a reviewer who may quote brief passages in a review.

First Edition
ISBN 0-8212-2875-7
Library of Congress Control Number 2003112766

Bulfinch Press is a division of AOL Time Warner Book Group.

Design by Lance Hidy

PRINTED IN ITALY

PAGE ONE: BROADWAY
FRONTISPIECE: NEW DAWN
LEFT: JOHN F. KENNEDY

THE INFINITE ROSE

A rose is a rose.

It is also an invitation to enter into the heart of hearts.

Has it not always been an expression of love?

How many ways do I love you?

Come closer! Gaze into my petals.

You may know me, but there is more.

Wander among my colors.

Take a deep breath. Stay awhile.

This is the beginning of forever.

BROADWAY

ICEBERG

MORGENSONNE

PEARL DRIFT

CIRCUS PARADE

CUPCAKE

UNKNOWN HYBRID TEA

SOUTINE

RING OF FIRE

CAREFREE DELIGHT

NEW DAWN

GOLD MEDAL

QUEEN ELIZABETH

BRANDY

MINILIGHTS

MACMILLAN NURSE

UNKNOWN HYBRID TEA

ELECTRON

MME. JULES BOUCHÉ

GOLD MEDAL

MASQUERADE

DOUBLE DELIGHT

FIGURINE

PEACE

ST. PATRICK

SALLY HOLMES

BABY MICHAEL

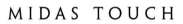

MIDAS TOUCH

PEACE

BROADWAY

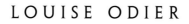

LOUISE ODIER

BABY MICHAEL

BLANC DOUBLE DE COUBERT

FIGURINE

LOVE

SEXY REXY

JOHN F. KENNEDY

KENTUCKY DERBY

CAREFREE BEAUTY

FRITZ NOBIS

GRACE DARLING

RUGOSA

JEAN GIONO

QUEEN ELIZABETH

KENT

RAINBOW NOISETTE

SUMMER FASHION

RED ROSE

SARAH VAN FLEET

FIGURINE

AMBER QUEEN

OHIO BELLE

OVERLEAF

SUMMER FASHION